D1241352

ELGIN BAYLOR

PAT RILEY

VERN MIKKELSEN

SHAQUILLE O'NEAL

JERRY WEST

KAREEM ABDUL-JABBAR

MAGIC JOHNSON

GEORGE MIKAN

EDDIE JONES

WILT CHAMBERLAIN

KOBE BRYANT

JAMES WORTHY

THE HISTORY OF THE LOS ANGELES LAKERS

CREATIVE EDUCATION

JOHN NICHOLS

Published by Creative Education, 123 South Broad Street, Mankato, MN 56001

Creative Education is an imprint of The Creative Company.

Design and Art Direction by Rita Marshall

Photos by Allsport, AP/Wide World, NBA Photos, SportsChrome

Library of Congress Cataloging-in-Publication Data

Nichols, John, 1966- The history of the Los Angeles Lakers / by John Nichols.

p. cm. – (Pro basketball today) ISBN 1-58341-102-X 1. Los Angeles Lakers (Basketball team)—History—

Juvenile literature. [1. Los Angeles Lakers (Basketball team)—History. 2. Basketball—History.] I. Title. II. Series.

GV885.52.L67 N53 2001 796.323'64'0979494—dc21 00-064540

First Edition 9 8 7 6 5 4 3 2 1

LOS ANGELES, CALIFORNIA, IS A CITY KNOWN FOR ITS SPRAWLING SIZE. THE CITY AND ITS SURROUNDING communities are spread over an area nearly 50 miles wide. Los Angeles's warm climate and beautiful setting between the San Gabriel mountains to the east and the Pacific Ocean to the west have lured people to the "City of Angels" for more than 200 years.

Home to Hollywood's movie and television studios, Los Angeles is also a place where the stars come out even in the daytime. In 1960, Los Angeles added another form of entertainment when the National Basketball Association's (NBA) Minneapolis Lakers decided to move to

VERN MIKKELSEN

southern California. The franchise already had a rich tradition of winning, so the team kept the name, becoming the Los Angeles Lakers.

Guard Herm Schaefer helped the Lakers win their division by 13 games in **1947–48**.

{CHAMPIONS IN THREE LEAGUES} The Lakers' story began in 1947. The franchise started out as a member of the National Basketball League (NBL), and its big star was a 6-foot-10 and 245-pound giant named George Mikan. Though he looked studious in his wire-rim glasses, Mikan was a terror on the court. With the big center manning the pivot, the Minneapolis Lakers easily won the 1948 league championship. "George was the game's first great big man," said Boston Celtics coaching legend Red Auerbach. "He was so big and strong, and yet he moved like a cat."

The next year, Minneapolis jumped to a rival league, the Basketball Association of America (BAA). To the surprise of no one, Mikan and the Lakers powered their way to a second consecutive championship. In

MAGIC JOHNSON

LAKERS
32
DALLAS
32

George Mikan, the NBA's first star, drew sellout crowds everywhere the Lakers played.

GEORGE MIKAN

1949–50, the NBL and the BAA merged to form the NBA, and the Lakers became the new league's elite team. Mikan was still the centerpiece, but Minneapolis also featured talented forward Vern Mikkelsen and guard Slater Martin. In the NBA's first playoffs, the Lakers waltzed through the early rounds, then topped the Syracuse Nationals in the Finals to claim the very first NBA championship.

Clyde Lovellette did his best to replace Mikan in **1955–56**, averaging 21 points a game.

After center Clyde Lovellette joined the team, the Minneapolis Lakers went on to win three more NBA titles in the next four years. Before the 1954–55 season, Mikan retired, and the Lakers' championship run came to a halt. By the end of the 1957–58 season, the Lakers had sunk to last place, and their popularity in Minnesota waned. Not even the addition of high-flying guard Elgin Baylor in 1958 sparked fan interest. By 1960, the Lakers were looking for a new home.

CLYDE LOVELLETTE

LAKERS
LAKERS

Pat Riley, who would later become the team's coach, began his Lakers career as a guard.

PAT RILEY

{THE LAKERS HEAD WEST} Before the 1960–61 season, the Lakers moved to Los Angeles, where a 14,000-seat arena promised the financial stability that the team needed to improve. That year, the Lakers also drafted guard Jerry West from the University of West Virginia.

The Lakers averaged 121 points a game in **1967–68**, setting a team record that still stands.

West and Baylor quickly became one of the league's deadliest backcourt duos. Baylor's explosiveness off the dribble and acrobatic drives to the basket were complemented by West's lethal long-range shooting and all-around game. "If you sat down to build a perfect 6-foot-3 basketball player, you would come up with Jerry West," said Lakers coach Fred Schaus.

Thanks primarily to West and Baylor, the Lakers began to dominate the NBA's Western Division. Five times in the years between 1962 and 1968, the Lakers captured the Western Division crown and squared off

ELGIN BAYLOR

against the Eastern Division champion Boston Celtics in the NBA Finals. Although Baylor and West gave brilliant performances, the Celtics went home with the title every time.

Needing a talented big man to help West and Baylor, Los Angeles traded forwards Archie Clark, Darrall Imhoff, and Jerry Chambers to the Philadelphia 76ers in 1968 for future Hall of Fame center

Wilt Chamberlain—the most feared player in the league. The 7-foot-1 and 275-pound Chamberlain had once scored 100 points in a single game during the 1961–62 season.

The Lakers missed the **1969** NBA title by two points, losing to Boston in the seventh game.

The Lakers and their trio of stars made two more runs to the NBA Finals in the next three years, but they came up short each time. Many experts said that the Lakers' stars did not possess the chemistry necessary to win a championship. Before the 1970–71 season, the 36-year-old Baylor decided to retire. "Elgin was such an amazing player," said West. "It's an embarrassment that we never won a championship with him."

The 1971–72 season finally brought an end to the Lakers' frustration. Although the team was without Baylor, forward Harold "Happy" Hairston and guards Gail Goodrich and Pat Riley stepped up to carry the load. The determined Lakers won 69 regular-season games, including an

WILT CHAMBERLAIN

LAKERS
13
CELTICS

NBA-record 33 in a row. Chamberlain concentrated on rebounding and defense and let West, Goodrich, and Hairston do much of the scoring. This team effort led to another trip to the NBA Finals. This time Los

Angeles broke through, beating the New York Knicks in five games. "This city's been waiting a long time," said Chamberlain. "It's a great feeling to be a champion."

{MAGIC PRESENTS SHOWTIME} After a few more seasons, both Chamberlain and West retired. Without their stars, the Lakers were still a good team, but not a great one. Goodrich and forward Connie Hawkins and guard Lucius Allen kept the team on a winning path, but the Lakers were no longer considered a true contender for the title.

Jerry West, the franchise's all-time leading scorer, was named to the All-Star Game in 14 seasons.

Before the 1975–76 season, the Lakers made a blockbuster trade for another outstanding big man, acquiring All-Star center Kareem Abdul-Jabbar from the Milwaukee Bucks for four players. "To win championships, you need a great center," said Lakers coach Bill Sharman. "And Kareem is as good as it gets."

In the late '70s, the Lakers began to build around their big man, acquiring high-scoring forward Jamaal "Silk" Wilkes from the Golden State Warriors and drafting point guard Norm Nixon. However, the final

JERRY WEST

LAKERS
17

The Lakers are known for their flashy style, but they have excelled through hard work.

piece to the Lakers' championship puzzle came in the 1979 NBA Draft, when Los Angeles chose 6-foot-9 guard Earvin "Magic" Johnson with the first overall pick. The charismatic Johnson was tall and strong enough to play forward or center, but he was also a brilliant passer and ball handler. With Johnson running the point, the Lakers played a dazzling, fast-break style that came to be known as "Showtime."

Speedy reserve guard Michael Cooper was a top defensive stopper in the **'80s**.

In 1979–80, the resurgent Lakers roared to a 60–22 record and cruised through the first two rounds of the postseason. In the NBA Finals, they met the Philadelphia 76ers and their superstar, Julius Erving. Los Angeles took a three-games-to-two lead in the series, but Abdul-Jabbar suffered a sprained ankle in game five and was forced to sit out game six. With his team shorthanded, the 20-year-old Johnson put on an amazing performance, scoring 42 points and grabbing 15 rebounds to

MICHAEL COOPER

lead the Lakers to a 123–107 game six victory and the NBA championship. "Magic was amazing tonight," said Lakers guard Michael Cooper. "Sometimes it's hard to believe he's just a kid."

{TEAM OF THE '80s} Los Angeles returned to the Finals again in 1982, and again its opponent was the 76ers. The Showtime Lakers, led by new head coach Pat Riley, beat Philadelphia in six games again to claim the franchise's eighth NBA championship. Riley, a key member of the Lakers' 1972 championship team, instilled a disciplined approach in his players and worked them hard in practice. "I never had a three-hour practice in my life until Pat got here," laughed Magic Johnson. "He works us like dogs, but the finished product is so pretty."

Forward Jamaal Wilkes quietly averaged 18 points a game during his Lakers career.

In the 1980s, the Lakers continued to play pretty basketball, but they also developed a killer instinct under Riley. The young coach drove his teams to not only win, but dominate. By the 1984–85 season, Riley preached this philosophy to a lineup that included Johnson and fellow guard Byron Scott, forwards James Worthy and Jamaal Wilkes, Abdul-Jabbar, and key reserve guard Michael Cooper and forward Kurt Rambis.

Los Angeles's depth was the deciding factor in the 1985 NBA

JAMAAL WILKES

Kareem Abdul-Jabbar displayed his trademark "Skyhook" in Los Angeles for 14 seasons.

KAREEM ABDUL-JABBAR

LAKERS
42

Finals, when the Lakers met the Boston Celtics. The Lakers were crushed 148–114 in game one, but they used their superior bench lineup and a huge effort from the 38-year-old Abdul-Jabbar to battle back and defeat the Celtics in six games. The championship victory was the Lakers' first Finals win in nine tries against the Celtics. "It is very sweet," said Riley. "Lakers fans have been waiting for this one a long time."

James Worthy, known for his clutch performances, won three titles with the Lakers.

The Lakers went on to win two more NBA championships in the '80s, beating the Celtics again in 1987 and topping the Detroit Pistons in 1988. Throughout the decade, the team received strong efforts from key players such as forwards Mitch Kupchak, Mychal Thompson, and A.C. Green, but it was primarily the nucleus of Worthy, Abdul-Jabbar, and Johnson that carried the Lakers to a decade-long run of excellence and took the popularity of pro basketball to new heights.

JAMES WORTHY

After the 1988–89 season, Abdul-Jabbar retired. The next year, Riley stepped down as head coach. Johnson and Worthy continued on and, with the help of Scott and new center Vlade Divac, led the Lakers

to another NBA Finals appearance in 1991. However, that year the team of the '80s faced what would be the team of the '90s: the Chicago Bulls. The Lakers won game one, but the Bulls roared back to take the next four and claim the title.

Early in the 1991–92 season, Johnson shocked the basketball world by announcing his retirement. The three-time NBA Most Valuable Player had tested positive for the HIV virus and decided to leave the game. Johnson attempted several comebacks over the next few seasons and even served as the team's head coach in 1994. Unfortunately, none of the experiments worked out. At the end of the 1993–94 season, the Lakers missed the playoffs for the first time in 18 years.

Guard Byron Scott was a valuable long-range shooter during the Lakers' glory years.

{SHAQ BRINGS SHOWTIME BACK} The Lakers' playoff drought lasted only one season. By the end of the 1995–96 campaign, Los Angeles was on the rise again. The team had brought in young players such as speedy swingman Eddie Jones and point guard Nick Van Exel to complement such veterans as Divac and forward Elden Campbell. The Lakers

BYRON SCOTT

were winning again, but they were not a serious title contender.

In 1996, the Lakers made two spectacular moves. The first was the signing of free agent center Shaquille O'Neal. The second was a draft-day trade that sent Divac to the Charlotte Hornets for the rights to Kobe Bryant, an 18-year-old high school swingman. "We've made these moves to prepare for championships in the present and in the future," explained team vice president Jerry West. "Shaq can help us immediately, and Kobe, we think he's going to be a great player in the near future."

Nick Van Exel led the Lakers in three-pointers for the fourth straight season in **1996–97**.

West proved to be correct on both counts as the Lakers stormed to a 56–26 record in 1996–97. The 7-foot-1 and 305-pound O'Neal averaged 26 points and 12 rebounds a game, while rookies Bryant and guard Derek Fisher made key contributions. The maturing Lakers went 61–21 a year later, but the team's youth and inexperience were evident in the

NICK VAN EXEL

playoffs. The Lakers were knocked out of the postseason by the Utah Jazz for the second year in a row.

During the 1998–99 season, the Lakers made another blockbuster trade, sending Jones and Campbell to the Charlotte Hornets for a pair of forwards, J.R. Reid and All-Star Glen Rice. Despite the additions, the Lakers were eliminated in the Western Conference Finals by the eventual NBA champion San Antonio Spurs.

In **1998–99**, Glen Rice was the only Lakers player to score at least 40 points in a game.

In 1999, Phil Jackson, the former coach of the six-time champion Chicago Bulls, came out of retirement to lead the Lakers. Jackson immediately put his stamp on the team, bringing in former Bulls guard Ron Harper and installing the complicated triangle offense that the Bulls had used. The Lakers responded to Jackson's new philosophy and breezed to a 67–15 mark. In the playoffs, the Lakers battled to the Finals, where

GLEN RICE

SHAQUILLE O'NEAL

Shaquille O'Neal dominated opponents in **1999–00** as he earned league MVP honors.

True to Lakers tradition, swingman Kobe Bryant was known for his dazzling moves.

KOBE BRYANT

they faced the Indiana Pacers. The veteran Pacers put up a fierce battle, but behind O'Neal's 41 points in game six, Los Angeles captured its 12th NBA title. "This is why I came here," proclaimed O'Neal. "I wanted to be a champion."

For more than 50 years, the Lakers have been one of the NBA's most consistently powerful franchises. With 12 NBA titles and a long tradition of excellence, the team's standard of success is sky-high. Lofty goals are only fitting, however, for a city where Showtime is king and the stars shine bright even in the daytime.

Horace Grant helped Shaquille O'Neal in the low post with his strong rebounding and defense.

HORACE GRANT